arias for
emma

words by eric sandor

Clink
Street

London | New York

Published by Clink Street Publishing 2020

ISBN: 978-1-913340-52-0 Hardback
ISBN: 978-1-913340-53-7 Ebook

For my beloved

Emma Sandor
11th October 1970 to 25th November 2016

I miss you beyond words

I will love you forever

words

foreword

Emma Cranfield and I met and fell in love when I was 18 years old. We were married 6 years later and celebrated our 20th wedding anniversary a month before she passed away. She is, and will always be, the love of my life. Losing Emma was more painful than I ever could have imagined. The poems in this collection were written in the midst of some of my deepest moments of sorrow. They are the honest, unfiltered words from a heart that has been crushed by grief and is attempting to heal. Writing, reading, and re-reading these poems has helped me work through the trauma of losing a loved one that is woven into the fabric of my being. My hope is that they may help others do the same. If nothing else, they are a lasting testimony of how much I love my precious wife and how much I have grieved her passing.

Eric Sandor
25th November 2019

yin

She sang

    sweet, soft notes that brushed his cheeks
    refrains of life drifting skyward
    lifting high the lowest chin
    paling the darkest part of a soul
    hailing their love and reveling in the light

of his yang before she left.

The abyss echoes low.
He collapses into its mouth
falling headlong, slow
erosion of his skin
by vacant sounds of air pressing past
until at last, he dares to sing
cracked, crooked lines,
croaked through plaintive sobs
into the void she left.

He sang

    ancient stanzas, wailing,
    railing against the moontide
    that ravages and creates
    that takes and breaks
    the deepest part of a soul
    starved staves, craving
    the clamor of noontime, praying
    for a din to drown the soundless air
    weighing stale upon his chest, yearning
    for her yin to show afresh
    among the shadows

of his yang before she left.

spectrum

All colors are scarred. Marred forever by her memory.

A fractured rainbow cut short in lament.
Bare and split, broken and rift
into hollow solitaires of mourning that question and curse.
Each tone, bent over at the middle in travail
like a row of kneeling tulips.
And a single pillar of dust remains
a monument standing in hushed query
too easily silenced, too swiftly dispersed, too blithely lost
in the wind of the wake
of the back of his hand.

grey

Who is the cold wind that blows
and the cat that climbs across my mind
meowing and howling at each other
across the grey ground
with its scars and troubles?

Scratching and hatching
mismatched memories
of faultless love lost
amidst a mess of severed veins.

Who's the author, the revealer, the reconciler?
Who's the smoother, the smotherer, the concealer?
Black and white smeared in the mud.
And rain falls. Fills the crevices. Covers the crevasses.

A dead grey bird lies listless and hidden on the turf.
A lifeless lovesong etched
in the contours of his palm.
A lonely landscape of loss
where the cat claws
new pathways and valleys
and the confused wind howls cold over the ridge.

white

Why does the white star stare at my feet
and whine like a mule in heat,
while I glare at the sheet lined without words?

She isn't morning or night.
Pure, hot, and empty,
she sings crooked stanzas.
She stands frozen.
Daring me to span
the endless sea that overwhelms.

Unwritten, she screams aloud
while the furnace burns cold
for the forger of fates.

Devoid of pigment.
Fortunes shot down for a clownfish supper with fools.

A bleak stone stands
scarred with white
bearing witness to what was,
and I remember the fullness of the past
    our first kiss, under the stars on Bristol's windward downs
    your red lips full of blood and heat, pressing on mine
    our youthful love rising in Paris,

as we cried and held each other to hide
your generous sighs, your open arms,
your forgiving smile
our firstborn's eyes, quizzing yours for some kind of reply
and how I gave you my heart with no thought for the future
but what remains now?

White writes, lights and ignites
but stops whiplashed.

Pale and hollow, she stands
and stares into vacant lands,
and waits…   white waits.

black

Where is the record of your destruction
that haunts the night
with lonely shrieks
while sheiks' wives wear their daily black?

Where's the recognition in the ashes
of our love, and of the perdition
slipped into the script
and slapped across the typeface?

Where do the Greek widows
get shade for their tears,
while witches' hats fall on rotten leaves
and my pupils narrow with hate
as the murderous crab crawls onward in the darkness?

Blindness suffered foolish schemes.
Scienceless,
evil overcame love in the midst of hope and faith.

Moonless,
the night rules unrestrained over my days
and everything's absorbed,
everything's absent,
everything is turned to black.

red

Pumped full of questions,
she storms wild,
while I punch my chest —
pleading for something more than blood.

Eyes wrung and wrecked.
Cheeks streaked,
wreaked by a slain heart.
The color of love burned
in the oven of grief.

Sun-shielded-shut eyelids
fail to snuff the crimson
that ceaselessly crows,
"I'm alive".

She pulses purposelessly, mercilessly on
and I drain red.

blue

The ache of your absence
swells into breakers
amidst a bare blue expanse.

Tides govern my breath,
besiege my dreams
while undertows surround me.

Your photo glimmers at my bedside.
Sitting smiling on a Cornish cliffside
where we had laid hidden on a soft ledge of long grass
beyond the precipice, unsurveyed
by all but the sea.

You are there, still. Surrounded by a silver frame.
A gift you gave me,
full of fresh young love,
yearning with a message carved with flowers beneath
"Forget-me-not".

I track your eyes in my sleep.
Your irises, that always told the truth.

I remember the years I lingered there
splashing down the cobalt paths
surfing the aquamarine streaks
playing hopscotch on the sapphire flecks
that were always kind
and always stretched to mine.

Now your eyes are midnight
cerulean shadows bled to black
and I do remember my love…
all too well…
but still, you are gone
and I am undone
by the blue of your eyes
and your forget-me-nots.

yellow

Yellow cries

Where did she go?

Daisy chains
and buttercup bracelets
spell out a distress call
and collectively bellow

Where did she go?

The daffodils I would bring home from work in Spring
now only shout together in chorus

Where did she go?

Dawn's light shines out gold
spreading fear and lies across the land.
Tarantulas wear bowties and dance with disdain
while pig scraps rot in the morning sun.

And no one,
anywhere,
can fathom the pain of yellow.

Where did she go?

time

Boulders fall as atoms raging

marking
>> the onslaught of the future
>> the consumption of the present
>> the loss of the past

measuring
>> cause and effect
>> the speed of our death
>> the distance between us.

Binding and breaking hearts
forming memorials and memory-loss
ticking off tocks and empty lists
to fill the void.

Rotten, rusted, ripened, matured.
An ingredient for better or for worse.

Best before, to have now, or to hold and cellar.

Fading light spreads
accruing wealth and debts
telling fortune's lies
darkening the freedom of the skies
with a sentence of life.

As there's no more time for you,
is there no more time for us?
If time itself were banished,
would your death vanish
and could I hold your hand again
and sing your name forever?

The duplicated expanse from sunrise to dusk
conspire together and the weight
of each day accumulate
time. The distance between us.

space

Crumpled, crowded and cramped.
Cornered and pressed
beyond your capacity to withstand any more,
and then it comes.

Another wave.
A rising tide of confounding confusion.
Overwhelming sadness floods and overtakes.
The vacuum of loss suffocates.
The emptiness surrounds in a siege.
Tempting and taunting, attempting to break you.
Sirens sing: You can close your heart.

Will you say, "enough" and hide inside the small space,
your mind's invitation to pretense and to become a shadow
   of yourself?

But I open my soul to the onslaught.
Defiant. Unyielding. Refusing the relief of lies.
I bare my chest, and face the firing squad.
And remain me.

It's cruelty offends.
The base, dreadful coldness
of forging a diamond
from the darkness of the soul.

There is no reprieve. No space to breathe.
The light of love laid siege by death.
Unrelenting clouds swarm.

I endure the downpour.
I choke and splutter, but through it all,
I utter, "I will overcome".

And there's a glimpse of beauty.
The human spirit, true and free.
And then darkness returns.

Cornered.
Pressed in the furnace.
I await the promised gem
and the light and space
to enjoy life again.

past

True to form, she broke down.
Reliable like cancer,
she had nothing left to give.
Used up and tossed aside like a soiled tissue.

My only love has passed away.

How could my love
be disposed of
like material?

She had wealth to give. She had life to live.
She had smiles, and eyes,
and ideas, and emotion.

She lost movement. She lost sight. She lost sound.
She lost her mind.
And then she lost her breath.

My only love has passed away.

I kissed her forehead for the last time.
It was cold and unfamiliar. I had lost her.
It was the last time I touched her.
Only seconds had past since she breathed her last.

And I cried. My first
tears of the rest of my life.
The years
stretching out to the horizon.
But she had none. No more time.
No more life. Dissipated like dust.
Ashes lost to the past.

I step forward through each second.
Plodding through thin air, I gasp
and grasp for something to hold.
My only love has passed away, while I will grow old.

Without her, is only pain.
Smiles are distorted and laughs are choked.
My veins are flooded with darkness.

My only love has passed away.

ending

Fire flies orange
down the sky.
Our sun, large, in charge
slowly sets
radiating hope for rest
with no thought of morning.

The day beyond the coming night
does not exist.
The moment dominates.
Suspended admiration
of the ending.

A crippled parade
a drama of colour
commands full attention.
All stop to pay homage
to her passing
and then move on.

Our life source wanes,
darkness envelopes brief hope
chased by panic
and all thoughts race frantic
for light.
But there is none.

Her memory
burned in our retinas
hovers quiet.
Absence deafens
smothers all thought and sound.

A frozen snow overwhelms the earth
hijacks plans and isolates
everyone
in thick darkness.

history

She turned her pages until her last note.

How can that be all?

I long to write more
for her story is so unfinished.
So cut short.
And all she was, is now his story.

How can that be all?

He tells their children of
     her exquisite grace
     her exceeding greatness
     her exemplary character
     her all excelling love for them.

How long til they forget?
How long til they neglect
and don't care to listen?

How much will he forget?
How much will he neglect
to include of her in his story.

She was so much more than her days.
She was so much more than his words.
She was so much more.

How can that be all?

He is so full of regret.
All he could have said, could have done.
The tiredness, desperation and waste of her last days, choke
   him still.

How can that be all?

And like everything, tears smear and evaporate and leave
    nothing but history.

No one cares for the past
but still
he tells his story
and sings
cries
sighs
about their love
and how extraordinarily unique she was.

clock

I close my eyes
and see her face.
Clear, like the first time
when we fell in love.

We walked together
in the garden in Cardiff.
I composed a rhyme around the face of the clock tower
that stretched above us, as we held hands:

"When the clock struck one,
my love for you had just begun…"

And I knew I loved you.
You laughed and giggled,
but I knew. I loved you.
And I feel that moment now,
back in time. My first love.
Like it was minutes ago.

I access the moment readily.
Like opening a drawer.
But you're gone. Far from me.
Beyond reach and stretch and all my yearning.
And yet you're here in my past.
In my heart's song.

And the pain is a mountain's weight
upon my chest. Suffocating me.
I catch my breath between wails
to no avail. There is no relief.
No quiet place of recovery.

I am so bereft. So split in two. I have lost everything.
Everything.
And I feel every inch of the loss.
Nothing is unaccounted for.

Oh my love! Come back to me!
I have no breath left, and no hope.
You are dead and I am undone.

I love you still.
It's overwhelming.

Time has been wiped away
and I suffer each breath without you.

There is no end to my tears or my sorrow.
I love you always and forever, my Emma.

face

I hold your face in my hands.
Touch your nose with mine.
Sink into your eyes.
Then open mine,
and you fade.

I hold your face in my hands.
All the force of my love
concentrated and focused
on you, on the moment.

I hold your face in my hands.
Intimate and familiar,
the creases and folds
of my palms wrap around
your cheeks and jawbone
and you're gone
into the air.

There is no thing so lovely,
no sight so pleasing and perfect
so completely adored
as your face.

I miss you more than breath.
Your absence. Your death
is a crater carved within my depths.
Your face is all that's left
and I hold it in my hands.

pain

Heartache, sorrow, pain.
A hard rain that drives
against my troubled heart
with incessant assaults.

Hollowness and shadows plague me.
Stalk my every move.
Cut down by snipers' crosshairs.
Lifeless and still, I moan.

Unrelenting.
There is no end.
Wave upon wave.
Trouble and despair wage war
through day and night.
There is no cure. No relief.

The agony of my distress
unbounded as the darkness
a piercing, bludgeoning, smothering hurt,
demands surrender.

Pain flows through me.
Undiminished. Unhindered. An endless force.

Gnawing. Clawing. Consuming. Crushing.
Chewing me to pulp. Compacting me as waste.

Pain sifts me into nothing.

leak

Sadness fills the house,
leaks through my pores.
Pours through my eyes.

An ache swells. Pregnant with harm.
Gives birth to death.

Dams burst. Shrieks of isolation
serenade the new moon.
To no avail.

The void surrounds.
Envelopes hope with emptiness.

Plagued with insurrection,
by assassins of affection.

Dread dominates and confounds.
Melancholy supersedes.
Health erodes and dissipates while hope leaks.
Leaving only desperation and loneliness and heart disease.

tear

You tear me open.
Raw flesh split deep.
A gaping hole
exposed
left.

Unresolved,
the tear weeps wide
moans long
sags and seeps soreness.

Tender to whispers
fragile to the breeze
it howls
stretched loose
more separated with every movement.

A bear shaped cloud
hangs heavy above me.
Black.
It threatens.
It beckons.
It engulfs
crashing oceans
on jagged coastlines.
It slowly swallows me.

A moonscape crater
in darkness,
the tear waits
unattended
deserted
undone.

wound

Her death carved a dark hole.

A vacuum of love
filled with violent doves.

Cooing.

Consuming the whole.
Swarming and gnawing
through organs and flesh.

My lady.
I lost her melody,
acquired a malady
of wakeful, painful, emptiness.

Her beauty. Her soft love.
My wound. Turned.
Afire with septic birds
flapping, swirling,
raging with their savage wings.

The darkness grows,
leaches sickness and heat.
An absence that makes the heart
suffer, weaken and splutter.

Breathless.
Squeezed and strangled.
Crushed to mush.
Unable to pump life any longer.
It's over.

And all that remains
are sharp wings
that fan and slap,
slice and flutter.

pressure

When it seems that all that can fall apart, has
and no crutch remains.

When all you have lived for is under threat,
and those you love, hover on a knife's edge.

When a valley of darkness overtakes and overwhelms,
and all hope for tomorrow has fled.

When no friend can help you, and no words bring solace.

When discouragement swarms, and taunts fly.
Speculation, intimidation, and cries of woe surround you.

Will you stand?
Still?

Will you
defy the storm that rages
square up to the eyes of your enemies?

Will you
refuse to give yourself to the jackals
refuse to be fodder for vultures?

Never surrender. Never give up. No matter how intense
the pressure.

Fight with every breath
forge your own future
write your story upon the world
and don't be fooled.
Don't imagine anything to be predetermined.

Reject everyone's will. Instead, impose your own.
Give yourself completely to your cause, and without
    mercy, kick it in the balls,
and in your heart utter, "screw 'em all".

Then you'll be a man my son.

relief

There is none.

No time for breath.
       No break for repose.
              No respite from the pain.

Constant erosion. Continuous corrosion. Unrelenting
   absence.

There is no way out.
There is no way round.

I push through the storm and sewer of remorse,
choking on love
vomiting from withdrawal
suffocating in loss.

Separate. I am destroyed.
Disassembled yin from unhinged yang.
A shadow undone by fleeting light.

No one comes to save or deliver.

I am just   abandoned dust.

Arid and useless
             without value
                      without redemption
                              without life.

Just a flea circus built upon a dream.

A mirage that offers
             no solace
                      no restoration
                            no relief.

dream

I don't
anymore

monotone and monochrome
without form or function

monopolized by monotony
without inspiration

monocles and monocycles
without vision or ambition

monosyllabic monograph
without point or purpose

monistic monogram, monolithic monologue
without companion

monogamy without compare
none-ogamy now

comatose
anaesthetized
stupefied
and nullified

I don't
anymore.

slurry

Sludge, fudge, and fury
messiness and curry.
Sloppy, spineless, and weak without his woman.

She was strong. True. Resolute.
A clear clarion call to action. To order.

Formless chaos cloaked in shadows.
Gelatinous, aimless, altogether less
without her.

A snowdrift.
A slow shift
to poverty
to absolute loss.

He cries himself empty
to no one
to no avail
to nothingness.

She has fled.
His heart has bled all.
It ceases to function.
It simply pretends.

There is no point in pumping, no hope in tomorrow.
Today is loss and hereafter is misery.

Structure is pointless.
A windfall of misfortune
cut off every route home
blocked any way of escape.

He suffocates in tears
drowns in sorrow and nears
life's hollow end.

one

How can one proceed?
Alone.
How could you concede?
You're gone.

An odd sock, a misplaced glove.
Unbalanced scales
that tell a tale of absence
and unrequited love.

I heard your heart stop silent
as I touched your face.
We fell out of stride.
I missed one step and fell.

Asymmetrical,
my heart limps out a new rhythm.
Every other beat, swept away
on a thick foamy tide of blood.

One beat remains, hunchbacked,
misshapen and burdened.
Slowly tapping out an un-received message.

The knot was undone
there is only one.

Odd and misplaced
one member of the pair
a monument to what was
and the other is lost
from time and space.

sorrow

Parting.

Our last touch
my kiss on your forehead, cold
with death not five minutes old.

You had gone.

Still, I should have lingered. Should have stayed.
Should have kissed you all over your face
and body. Should have laid on top of you
and held you tight
and squeezed your head against mine
and stayed.

You had gone.

The world was ruptured in two
like my ears from the sonic boom
of your passing.

And you had gone.

I should have shouted down the cancer,
should have forbidden it,
banished it from your body.
I should have prevented its rise,
incited an attack on me instead.

I should have blackmailed the nurses and doctors,
threatened them with their lives,
offered them all my possessions
to keep you alive.

I should have held you longer. Pried open your eyes.
Slapped your face and pumped your heart and lungs.
Shaken you by the shoulders and shouted in your ears,
to please stay. But you had gone.

Parting is such deep sorrow.

kiss

I miss your kiss.

I miss
your face, your sound, your eyes, your arms.

I miss
your wit, your laugh, your sweetness, your grace.

I miss
your love, your strength, your smile, your style.

I miss
your time, your hands, your cheeks, your touch.

I miss
the shape of your head, your mouth, your nose.

I miss
giving you gifts, giving you lifts, lifting your lids at daybreak.

I miss
morning skies, sunrise on your skin, and temporary goodbyes.

I miss you Emma.

night

Sweetness slides home
by way of the North Star.
Sweeps aside love and smiles.

Lightness of spirit crawls past
the doorway to the cellar.
Charms friends and other reptiles.

Loneliness caresses the moon
and spans a black hole.
Ignites passion for the void.

Darkness strolls along corridors
that echo into chambers of the heart.
Sings lullabies to creatures of the deep.

When will I look upon a face of beauty,
kiss lips that love and long,
trip over my tongue in pursuit of perfection.

Something calls my name quietly
but meanly. Needling my ribs.
And sweetness and light fail
on my moonless starless nights.

proud

Trouble stirs while **Weakness** sits across the table from **Fear**,
his older brother. Boasting yet another
unaccepted challenge to arm wrestle.
The elder eyes the door, rapidly taps the dusty floor,
while the younger sucks musty air through blunt teeth.

Sorrow lays close, with his lover and friend.
Pleads with her to relent. For once, to be silent.
Unyielding, impatient, unrepentant,
Agony clears her throat. She stands proud,
and sings to her long-time companion, loud
cries of tortuous pain unending,
while all eyes stare, uncomprehending.

She stands proud, empty of all but grief.

Joy is a thief. Lurking in dark shadows
that obscure truth and justice.
She lies in wait for a sign, a cue,
some invitation to perform her dance, but there is none.

He reclines, heavy, at a loss.
Nostalgia. Fat and stubborn. Mouth agape for lost times
    with her.
Smiles of juveniles, loving in the long grass of summer
wriggling with soft sweet delight of skin on skin
missing no one, while kissing clouds goodbye.
And yet minds forget more than they fail to remember.

And all the while she stands proud,
wailing loud from sun to stars, suffering always
hour by hour.

Unwilling to complete her shift
to rest her head,
for her refrain to fade. Yes,
Agony stands proud, while all others sit in her shadow.

siren

Stars embrace your bosom
a flash streaks vast across the sky
no one knows where or why
no one cares.

No one dares to look today in the eye
but everyone stares
at the crisscrossed grave clothes
of yesterday.

The siren calls to scatter, to gather, to trap, to rescue.

I fall willingly
while the world turns in chaos
a mystery of existence
spinning in a vacuum.

Sucked in, tucked in, and
plucked from life like a wildflower.
Still, she calls him to come.

He must answer.
Yield to her charm.
Heed her alarm.
Stop short of liberty, and sacrifice all
for one more brush of her lips.

Lost, confused and displaced
damaged, ravaged, and misplaced,
he wanders aimless
and still, the siren calls
with echoes cold and long.
Hollow and uncertain
he falls.

dusk

In the desert twilight
there remains a shadow of fallen bones
contours of home and a glow of hope.

In the distance rolling low and shallow
veiled from view
she hums hallowed melodies of our youth
while cattle snort and grunt on hot dirt
and dogs bark hollow cries into the night air.

Above the hills beyond falls a stifled sound.
My love softly calls
for me to come
for me to rest my head
for me to join her in the clouds.

The moon and stars rise
and my eyes close.
Seeing all that's hidden
knowing the signs in the skies.

Pages turn
and seasons lapse
and still I yearn for hers
not to have passed.

Tomorrow is a fresh clean sheet
but is so hard to embrace
and so hard to erase the elephant's weight
of the truth that each new day
leaves her farther behind.

rise

A pin-prick of light, orange and pure
appears first.

An arc slim and bright, shines along the curve
of the horizon.

A hair's breadth, turning from black to pink
from death to birth.

Only the morning star remains standing,
tipping its hat in admiration
before it too retires.

The night watch sleeps
while a wedge of hot love
rises above the earth
illuminating, rejuvenating, resuscitating all.

Indiscriminately lavishing breath and light
and even I
can feel its rays of life and heat
deep beneath the heavy soil of my grief.

Nothing is beyond its reach, as it rises
in command,
to take its stand,
to obliterate from memory the atrocities of the night.

thaw

A dense blanket smothers
insulates me from pleasure
dulls, darkens, covers
my mind
suspends reality, space and time.

Frozen, I lay buried
under 5 foot 8 inches of grief
and sorrow
isolated from health and relief.

Then, a near imperceptible change commences.
A slightest return of the senses.

The darkness begins to offer shadows
muffled steps trouble the air
and frostbite's march is curtailed.
An inch of space emerges along my skin
a cessation of pressure and room to wriggle in
my self-made grave.

I twist and turn and press my weight against the thaw.
Ravenous for life
brawling for breath and fighting to be free
when, amidst the struggle I come to see,
I am.

goodbye

Some say see you later
some say see you soon
some last for decades
while others last for moons.

Some mean good riddance,
and kicking dust off feet
but one is worse than death; bereaved
of the love your soul completes.

Farewell, adieu, goodbye
pathetic words of empty breath
that fail to mark the pain of losing
your only love to death.

You never said goodbye my love
in texts or in your last hours
you simply left me xxx's
before they sent us flowers.

You didn't know I was at your side
didn't know to say goodbye.
I held your hand and stroked your head
while you suffered between breaths and said,

"Tell my sister I love her.
Tell the children I love them.
Tell Eric I love him."

The last words you spoke on earth
you didn't know I'd heard.
And I was there by your bed
praying as you left.

All at once, by your side,
I stood alone.
Didn't know how to say goodbye.
Just kissed you when you'd gone.

free

"Free…"

"Free… Free…"

The young bird cheeps in the tree
above the shade of the morning star.
I heard her sing,
but no one answered in the heavens.

"Alone… Alone…"
She echoes out
cold facts of her existence
chirping away life on the bough.

"Sleep… Sleep…
they say, this is no time to tweet…
but freedom isn't free…
and certainly wasn't cheap…

How will you survive… if you choose not to cry?
How will you recover… if you never strive
to learn the ways of life and death?

How will you ever fly above the clouds?
How will you ever sing loud enough to be heard?

How will you ever be free if you never say a word
about the way she left you?",
the thoughtful chick lectured.

I knew the sage was right.
It can never be wrong, even in grief
to sing a song of freedom
even when it costs you, your life.

touch

Soft clouds speak words of truth
utter promises to barren mountains; to bleak cliffs
stutter curses of affection to valleys of shame and regret
clutter the horizon, shutter the moon.

I long to be touched by the mists
a tender brush of hands and wrists
on derelict freckles, abandoned skin
cresting cracked curves of flesh,
held once again in secret trysts.

Rains renew and conclude. Pour life or death
on sinews, fire and sand
streams of portent that plead, demand
recourse or remedy for the unwashed land.

How can I sail across the chasm
soar home to your subtle charms
hold your frame in my arms
and kiss your irises amidst the storm?

Tasting shadowed garden paths
plaguing dreams of reunification
with screams of dissension
that you were the only one.

Beyond sight and hope
there rests a dove sleeping alone
with thoughts of reunion,
songs of home
and when we touch, I'll know.

mark

The mark you left is calling
in the eyes of our children
in the wound on my rib
in the colour of my dreams.

Your love overwhelms me still
the constancy of your smile
your loyalty and strength to stand
by me, regardless what I held in my hand
quietens my sobs in reverent thanks.

I never deserved you or your love
whole, free and clear,
you gave, and I embraced
an imbalanced deal
that juxtaposed your grace
with my roughshod soul

with only one consolation,
one route of escape, that
nowhere on earth could be found
anyone deserving of you,
my Emma.

You soared above your peers
with the perspective of miles
whispered wisdom of the years
to me, and all the while

others mistook your silence
for a lack of words
misjudged your humble kindness
for a lack of mighty strength.

No. You were far beyond their power
of imagination. Immortal, beyond our
boundaries and days.

How will I leave my mark upon the world?
For what purpose? With what effect?
Now that your voice is mine
how can I hope to resurrect
and harness all you possessed

to leave a monument of your name
a lasting mark of our unworldly love
across a vast mountain range
a treasure map visible from space
to lead future generations to freedom.

You were a divine composition
of constellations
of light years of stars
drawn together over aeons
into skin and bones
into blue eyes and bloodied heartbeat
for a few brief moments of breath.

Too swiftly consumed back to stardust
too greedily transformed back into
the vastness of the skies.

Earth couldn't hold your fire
but it was long enough
to forever mark my soul
and your voice cries out within me
to push that mark into the soil and mud
to engrave upon the rocks and grass
the brazen rebellion of everlasting love
flowing down the rivers and waterfalls
of generations to come.

gone

Not sunlight nor moon
nor expanse between
can erase or ease
the torment of the skies.

My soul stands alone
bereft and abandoned
my one true love is gone.

No amount of words can do you justice
no volume of breath can fill the abyss
no measure of tears or wails will ever smooth
my broken wilderness.

My soul sits alone
orphaned and abandoned
my one true love is gone.

Images of you delight and destroy
your face, forever unlined
your skin bronzed with youth
your feet frozen in the sky
your palms burned to dust in the blaze.

My soul lies alone
widowed and abandoned
my one true love is gone.

All remedies have failed
all strategies of salvage thwarted
all verses have fallen short and
can never join arms or stitch together
my frayed life.

eric sandor

My soul rests alone
derelict and abandoned
my one true love is gone.

enough

How much time will I spend trying to mend?
How much grief before I have relief?
How much pain will I have to know?
How many tears will flow?
How many years will pass before
your name brings only joy?

Why was your mind assailed with insanity?
Why did your grace endure such indignity?
Why did your muscles fail, and your eyes lose sight?
Why did your body give up the fight?
Why was I so unable to bring you home?
Why did you believe you died alone?

How much hurt can one heart survive?
How many more pieces can be broken
before it ceases to function?

How long will I carry the weight
of your hospice bed on my back?
How long will my head hang slack
with a vision of you diminished?
How long until this sorrow is finished?

How much further can I fall
before the point of no return?

How much, how many, how come,
how far, how long
is enough?

forever

Always constant, my love will last.
Never changing, my love will last.
Forever raging, my love will last.

Light years of constellations cannot endure,
cannot survive time.

While stars burn cold and dry
and comets dissolve to dust.

While oceans boil all life to death
a victim to heat and pressure.

Nothing can outlast my love for you, my Emma.
My love will last. That is sure.

Your name is a universe of its own,
consuming all matter, space, and time.
Your face, your voice, your essence.
Memories of you sweep away planets
leaving only our love.

When no life remains,
when empires collapse and species fail
my love will still be singing,
outlasting them all.

We will transcend
and overcome the impossible.

My love will last
forever and unstoppable.

9 781913 340520